LIVING AND LOVING

Selections from the Devotional Works of
PROFESSOR A. THOULUCK
For Every Day Of The Month

Edited and with Introduction by

Francis E. Clark, D.D.
Preisdent of the United Society
of Christian Endeavor

First Fruits Press
Wilmore, Kentucky
c2015

Living and loving: selections from the devotional works of Professor A. Tholuck for every day of the month, edited and with introduction by Francis E. Clark.

First Fruits Press, ©2015
Previously published: Boston, Chicago : United Society of Christian Endeavor ©1898.

ISBN: 9781621714156 (print), 9781621714163 (digital)

Digital version at http://place.asburyseminary.edu/christianendeavorbooks/6/

For all other uses, contact:

First Fruits Press
B.L. Fisher Library
Asbury Theological Seminary
204 N. Lexington Ave.
Wilmore, KY 40390
http://place.asburyseminary.edu/firstfruits

Tholuck, August, 1799-1877.
    Living and loving : selections from the devotional works of Professor A. Tholuck for every day of the month / edited and with introduction by Francis E. Clark.
    43 pages ; 21 cm.
    Wilmore, Ky. : First Fruits Press, ©2015.
    Reprint. Previously published: Boston : United Society of Christian Endeavor ©1898.
    ISBN: 9781621714156 (pbk.)
1. Devotional exercises. I. Title. II. Clark, Francis E. (Francis Edward), 1851-1927.
BV4834 .T52 2015

Cover design by Jonathan Ramsay

asburyseminary.edu
800.2ASBURY
204 North Lexington Avenue
Wilmore, Kentucky 40390

First Fruits
THE ACADEMIC OPEN PRESS OF ASBURY SEMINARY

First Fruits Press
The Academic Open Press of Asbury Theological Seminary
204 N. Lexington Ave., Wilmore, KY 40390
859-858-2236
first.fruits@asburyseminary.edu
asbury.to/firstfruits

LIVING AND LOVING

Selections from the Devotional Works of

PROFESSOR A. THOLUCK

FOR EVERY DAY OF THE MONTH

Edited and with Introduction by

FRANCIS E. CLARK, D. D.

*President of the United Society
of Christian Endeavor*

UNITED SOCIETY OF CHRISTIAN ENDEAVOR
BOSTON AND CHICAGO

2

CONTENTS

6 *CONTENTS.*

THOLUCK'S HOURS OF DEVOTION.

SOME authors exert a peculiar power upon their readers. Their books are no more learned or profound or witty or sparkling than the works of others, but they exert a fascination which at first cannot be altogether explained. These books attract one like the eyes of a speaking portrait, which follow him about the room and rest upon him wherever he stands.

If this power should be analyzed, I think it would be found that it is the *heart* quality of these books that lends to them their unusual attraction. They are written out of the heart of the author for the heart of the reader. They are not cold, mental abstractions. You would not say of them: "What a splendid *work!*" "What a fine literary *effort!*" In fact, they do not impress you as the result of effort. The element of labor is overshadowed by the element of inspiration. When you close the book, you do not say to yourself: "What a great mind has this author!" "What a prodigious monument to his industry and his intellect is this volume!" but, "What a great heart he has! how much he loves! how far he sees into the Unseen!"

Such a writer as this was Professor Tholuck, of Halle.

Of all devotional writers, ancient or modern, I know of none that appeals more directly to the *heart* of his readers. None speaks out of deeper personal experience, or draws therefrom more refreshing draughts of comfort. The reason for this is plain, for, as he himself tells us, his "Hours of

7

Devotion " were wrought out of his own personal and some-times bitter experience.

While he wrote, he himself was upon the anvil, being shaped by many a blow for the Master's use.

He writes not what he had learned from books, but what the great Graver had first written upon his own soul.

He tells us that in his early life he had not thought of laboring in the field of devotional literature, but in the year 1826, when bowed down both in mind and body by long and severe illness, he began to write meditations on passages of Scripture, chiefly with a view to his own consolation. This task, however, was never finished.

A few years afterwards his eyesight threatened to fail him, and it was then, during the winter mornings and evenings, when he was prevented from using his eyes by candle-light, that, in quiet meditation, the plan of these " Hours of Christian Devotion " was matured.

Thus the genesis of this volume is another illustration of the way in which all things work together for good to them that love God.

To lose his health, and then his eyesight, so that he feared he would be compelled to give up his professorship alto-gether, must have been a sore and grievous affliction to the good professor, but, during those hours of semi-darkness for mind and eye alike, God appeared to him ; God's light shone upon his heart, his spiritual vision was quickened, he caught glimpses of God and his love and of the eternal world, that his undimmed natural vision would have never beheld, and, because of these hours of gloom and sadness and broken health and shattered hopes, he has put the whole world under a debt of gratitude such as it owes to few writers in all the centuries.

In later years, writing of the composition of this volume, he says : " At the time, the danger of being compelled to resign for several years, if not forever, my vocation as pro-fessor was constantly present in my mind, and, if a season of affliction is not in general the most unfavorable for the production of a religious work, I may be permitted to indulge good hopes of the success of the present volume, as not only the original conception, but also the subsequent execution of it, occupied what were very grave hours in my life."

In these days we are not accustomed to go to Germany for our most profoundly spiritual and devotional books. We look to the Fatherland for speculative philosophy, for theology and criticism, but not often for books that speak to the heart of the simple and unlearned Christian. Yet here is a profound theologian, a scholar whose accuracy and erudition are acknowledged by all the world, who writes in language that a child may read and understand, if his heart has been touched by the love of God.

" The true theologian," declares Tholuck, " is he who, after climbing the ladder of science to a height at which he has the unclouded heaven in view, delights himself with gazing into it, and no longer thinks of the steps of the ladder save when employed in the friendly office of helping those at the foot to mount."

Professor Tholuck evidently sought to realize his own high ideal of a true theologian. He mounted the ladder of the mere science of theology until he could look into the unclouded heavens, and what he saw there, which it was lawful for him to utter, he has told to us, and has not wearied us with a constant obtrusion of the doctrinal rounds and philosophical rungs by which he climbed to his exalted view-point.

In his preface to the English translation of his famous volume, he well expresses the frame of mind in which his book was written. " Like the pious Tersteegen," he says, " I thought with myself, If my God does not will as I do, I will as he does, and thus we always keep on friendly terms. I also sought to extract a gratification from those hours of bitter suffering, by presenting to Christian souls a fruit of the heart in place of a labor of the head. . . . I have been young, but now am old; I have spent a whole lifetime in battling against infidelity with the weapons of apologetical science; but I have become ever more and more convinced that the way to the heart does not lie through the head, and that the only way to the conversion of the head lies through a converted heart, which already tastes the living truths of the gospel."

Tholuck's whole book is a commentary on this significant sentence. It is a book from the heart, of the heart, to the heart.

My difficulty has been great in selecting a few pages which the compass of this little volume allows from the nearly six hundred closely printed pages from which I had to choose.

It is difficult to tell whether Tholuck's poetry or prose is the more helpful. Almost every chapter in his volume is begun and ended with a little poem, which is a gem in itself. I have room to quote in this connection but two or three, but perhaps they will send my readers to the mine from which they came. Here is the fore-word of a chapter in regard to choosing God and his will, rather than one's own : —

> " 'I am so sad and care-oppressed ! '
> My friend, I well believe 't is true ;
> *I* should be quite as much distressed,
> Had I as many lords as you.
> Lightning and hail, and fire and storms,
> Cattle and neighbors, fowl and worms,
> Of monarchs what a train !
> For me I have one only Lord,
> And all that host fulfil his word,
> As body-guards the king obey ;
> And so I cast my cares away."

Above all does Tholuck speak to those who desire to come into the immediate presence of God. Every meditation takes one into the audience-chamber of the King. More than any other author whom I know does he seem to talk with God, and to reveal God to man. He opens the door into the infinite, and through the open door we see God only. God in the face of Jesus Christ, God in providence, God in his Word, God in his world, but always God.

As we read and meditate with the upward glancing eye of faith, there will come to us, I believe, emotions that must have thrilled the author when he wrote, emotions of joy, and confidence, and complete rest in the omnipotent One.

> "What means this throbbing at my heart,
>   So blissful and so new,
>   As if there were some open part,
>   And heaven were breaking through?
>   'T is even so ; close not the door,
>   And a whole ocean in will pour."

As the reader in the Quiet Hour feels this "throbbing at his heart," as he realizes that heaven is indeed "breaking through," and that the Morning Watch is as the door of heaven to him, may he be able fully to say with the heavenly-minded Tholuck : —

> "God is the fountain at which I drink,
>   God is the ocean in which I sink;
>   I gaze o'er the main, but no shore descry;
>   And helpless and feeble, alas! am I.

> "What then? Would I measure the flood immense?
>   No ; losing of self all thought and sense,
>   Undaunted the awful deep I brave,
>   And sink, and dissolve, like a drop in the wave.

> "Thy *thought*, like thy measureless *being*, no line
>   Can fathom, nor term nor bound confine.
>   Yet I feel no dread, for I think with delight
>   That thy *love* is as vast and as infinite."

FRANCIS E. CLARK

THE CENTRE OF MAN'S BEING.

ESUS, my Lord, truly dost thou say that souls which, like Martha, labor only for this world's meat, are careful and troubled about many things, and that the better part is that which Mary chose; for, since I began to hunger for the meat of heaven, my carefulness and trouble are greatly subdued, and now are always mingled with some sense of peace; whereas before, so long as I strove after earthly blessings and earthly wisdom alone, I was never free from restlessness and disquiet. But to the violent, who, with sword in hand, would make a conquest of thee, thou never yieldest. They only find who seek thee with child-like hearts. The millions of sunbeams that warm and cherish us come all of them at once, but all so softly and silently down; and even so dost thou desire to be sought, — earnestly, indeed, but not with hot and boisterous haste. Dear Lord! when Mary took her place at thy feet, thou didst sit down beside her; and to every soul that longs after thee thou wilt do the same. Thy only wish is to see us all at thy feet like her. From the silence that reigns in thy school, I used to think that life in a manner ceased when love to thee began; and, behold, I have found that " in loving thee I first began to live." So long as I was out of the centre I roved around the whole circumference of creation, and had no rest. I found the centre in finding God, and I need to wander about for rest no more.

THE HIDDEN MANNA.

LIGHT in the centre illumines the whole circumference; and even so, when there is grace in the heart, it radiates its brightness upon all man's outward employments. Martha then performs her service, but she does it with the mind of Mary. Holy Jesus! doubtless thy labor in the shop of Joseph was as much a worship as' thy prayers in the temple. It was ever thy meat to do thy heavenly Father's will, and with this hidden manna thou wert regaled even when standing at the carpenter's bench. And the same hidden manna shall also be my food, whether in my workshop or at my desk, whether laboring in the fields or walking in the streets.

> In every work, however mean,
> Some touch of heaven we trace,
> If but the heart within have felt
>   The influence of grace.
> And art and skill, beneath love's ray,
> Their choicest flowers and fruits display.

O Lord, rich in grace, when thou takest possession of the heart, how beautifully all the natural talents thou hast lent us expand! Beneath the sunny influence of thy love even our secular employments thrive and prosper. O, if they but knew, how would the men who only strive for success in temporal affairs take to heart what thy word avers, that "godliness is profitable unto all things, having promise of the life that now is, and of that which is to come"!

THE BEST MOMENT.

WHAT a moment is that in which a man for the first time hears and fully believes the Saviour's words, "Thy sins are forgiven thee"! Among all by whom it has been experienced, who has a tongue sufficiently eloquent to describe it to those to whom it is unknown? It is an exaltation, it is an abasement, and, at the same time, in both, a blessedness with which no other state can compare. Ye full and self-satisfied souls, would that you but knew the full import of the word "grace," — grace without desert!

Never has so mighty a *flood* of inward strength caught and borne me along on its wave as in those hours when, kneeling in the silence of my closet, I felt the Saviour's hand upon my head; and, as the best recompense of my tears, heard him say : —

> From all thy sins I thee absolve.
> Look on me, and believe and rise, my son;
> Be of good cheer, gird up thy loins, and run.

Yes; though before I had only crept, in that hour I obtained strength to run. Grasping his hand, the beloved hand that blessed me, I vowed this vow in his presence : —

> Yes, Saviour, both my hands I give
>   To seal the promise I renew;
> I 'll love thee only while I live,
>   And only live to serve thee, too.

THE EVERLASTING LOVE.

"THOU hast loved me with an everlasting love," for thy love is older than my life. Thou didst love me before I existed, for it was because thou didst love me that I now exist. Before the world was created thou didst call me by name, and thou didst create the world with an eye to me, the poorest of thy children, in order that, along with all the millions who at my side advance to the goal of consummation, I, too, might find a path to conduct me to the same.

O, what confidence, what fortitude, what magnanimity, are inspired by the thought that I, too, was thought of in this world of God, and that for me, among the rest, it was prepared! Brave and determined does the soldier enter the conflict, when he knows for certain that the general whose eye surveys the field has reckoned upon him also being at his post. Even though he fall, he knows he is in his right place. Like him, I, too, know that He whose eye of affection overlooks the universe has assigned to me my station, and traced out for me my path. Onward I march through perpetual vicissitudes of brightness and gloom, and the issue is as yet hidden from my view. But the eye that knows no change beholds it from eternity to eternity in a light that is ever the same.

DREAMERS AND SEERS.

WHENCE comes this certainty and confidence? It cannot have its source in the
sublunary world, and must be a testimony
vouchsafed by God to the soul. Let there
be but a grain of such inward faith, and it will remove
mountains of appetites and lusts, and extirpate the pas-
sions most deeply rooted in the heart. Yes, a single
grain of such faith makes the entire domain of visible
things transparent to us. We see through them all, and
taste through them all, the powers of the invisible
world to come. That "in him we live, and move, and
have our being," becomes a reality to the believer; and
the words of the Lord, " I am a God at hand, and not
afar off," a matter of experience. He scents the breath
of the Divine Being whether he walks forth into the
garden of nature, or mixes in the society of men, or
remains in the solitude of his closet. We need not
wonder that the generality look upon the believer as
a fool and a dreamer who lives in a world of his own,
instead of that which is common to the race. And yet
the reverse is the case. *They* are the dreamers. It is
they who live in a world of their own; for so long as the
breath of God is not everywhere traced and felt here
below, what is the world but the vain and unsubstantial
fabric of a dream? No, it is *we* who are awake; we
who now in time already experience eternity, and in the
present world taste the powers of that which is to come.

HOW GOD SPEAKS.

THERE are preachers in the firmament above, preachers in the earth below, preachers within us and preachers without. What a sermon it is which the firmament of heaven alone preaches to us, — the sky, whether azure and serene, or overcast with stormy clouds! The heaven, with its marvels, declares the glory of God by the magnificence of day as well as by the magnificence of night.

But do many listen? Can it be denied that until God speaks to his heart within, man cannot comprehend the language he utters from everything about and above and beneath him? How beautiful to this effect the words of Tauler! "He who gazes long at the sun sees a sun impressed on every object to which he afterwards turns his eye; and it is the same with him who is much occupied with the contemplation of God." There are hours when we can stand in the bosom of nature and feel as if we were in a church, and a fresh doxology were gushing from every breast, so that we cannot choose but join the hymn, and are caught and borne along by the general flood of devotion. At other times again, how dumb and speechless the creatures around us seem all to be, as if every one of them must needs pursue its way alone without the guidance of a heavenly hand! The difference depends upon whether God speaks within us or not.

Open thy heart to God; if he be there,
The outspread world will be thy book of prayer.

GOD'S BITTER CUP.

ALAS! it is no easy task to exercise a truly Christian faith in the Omnipotent. How clearly the unbelief of my heart reveals itself afresh whenever God is pleased to beset my path with thorns! We know and repeat to ourselves a thousand times, that, as the eternal wisdom, justice, and love is likewise omnipotence, it is able at every moment to execute what it wills. But notwithstanding, how hard we find it to believe that it is the will of God which calls us to *suffer* not less than when it calls us to *act!* We nourish the delusion that it is only the act lying *behind* the suffering, the freedom *behind* the fetter, which God wills, and not the suffering and the fetter, too. These, we fancy, have been interposed by some foreign hand; and in this manner we forego the blessing which the Lord intends afflictions and restraints and hindrances to convey. The idea that the divine omnipotence removes distress is one on which every man broods far longer than upon the thought that it is also divine omnipotence that *inflicts* it, and that there must have been as good grounds for *sending* as for *mending* it. Men are always saying, "God will soon make it well again." Why do they not as often say, "It was God who made it what it is"?

Think not that some *foe* the burden came,
    And all you owe to *God* is strength to bear it.
The cross, the curb, are his because the same
    Almighty power must will who could repair it.
Seek then, my child, thy Father's mind to know
    In what befalls thee, be it weal or woe.

GOD GREAT IN LITTLE.

E must be great in what is little as well as in what is large.

> The daisy on the mountain sod,
>   Withdrawn from human view,
> Was planted by the hand of God,
>   The hand that fashioned you.
>
> That flower his care protects whose call
>   Did countless worlds create;
> By condescending to the small,
>   He proves that he is great.

I will not, then, try to measure the eternal by the standard of my own little eye; and although, amidst the conflict of the forces and beings in the world, *my* ear has not as yet been opened to catch that harmony in which they all join, I yet will not dispute that it exists. I figure to myself a deaf man suddenly and for the first time brought within sight of a great orchestra, and observing the busy movements of the hands and feet, and the sweat upon the faces of the musicians, and all for nothing, and I reflect how absurd it would appear to him. We men occupy the same position with respect to the universe. O, when I shall one day know him even as I am known, and perceive through the vast creation the measure, number, and weight according to which all things are ordered, and how the least of them is connected and in concord with the greatest, what a blessed harmony it will be, and how it will regale my soul through all eternity!

GOD'S ANOINTING.

YES, only let God be mine, and let his presence refresh my soul, and I can be joyful in the face of all enemies. How a true and heartfelt sense of the nearness of God can often make us unspeakably calm and patient, even when our adversaries are raging most fiercely around! Seasons like these are hours of tuition which God gives to man, and the lessons which we then learn are never forgotten in all our future life. We then feel so independent of the world and of all the creatures, and as if we stood loose from everything else, and were solely in the hand of our God. Thus stood the Saviour before his judge when he answered him, " Thou couldst have no power at all against me except it were given thee from above." According to the Psalmist's description, a man is then as if he were sitting at a well-furnished board, his head anointed with oil, and drinking cup after cup of the peace of God, while his enemies are toiling and raging around him. Or, as Luther says of himself, "that amidst their noise and tumult he, in the name of his God, sat still and sung his hymn." The world cannot understand such resignation, and is often exasperated by it ; but sometimes also its hostility is thereby softened.

And how true, likewise, are the Psalmist's words with reference to *inward* adversaries! Even in our bosoms storms may rage, and yet in the face of all enemies the cup of consolation is filled for us to the brim. There is a host of foes in the believer's breast, but there is also a strong tower to which he can flee for refuge.

BEWARE OF EXCUSES.

HOW deep a seat do certain bosom sins acquire, which, although they seem only something ·isolated, — such, perchance, as impatience, self-will, want of order and punctuality, vanity, — still, if permitted to grow unchecked, threaten extinction to the infant life of the new man! The whole strength of the vine may run into two or three shoots, and make it unfruitful. A godly man has made the remark that by *deliberately* yielding to even one fault we subvert the whole fabric of Christianity, and that to do so is as when a master suffers a single rafter of his house to fall into decay. Now this is a matter in respect of which many Christians are under a delusion. We are less clear-sighted to our own darling sins than others are, who yet dare not tell them to us. And so many live on from day to day, the rafter all the while becoming more and more frail. The thought of this will sometimes suggest itself, and conscience begin gently to knock. But how quickly do a host of excuses, like the officious menials of some despotic lord, present themselves and exclaim, " Who knocks there? Silence ! " and all is quiet again. There is no task so hard as for a man to take arms against himself. Beware, then, of excuses. They perform the part of sponsors at the baptisms of the devil.

> Far-stretched pretexts and reasonings
> Are fickle and deceptive things :
> Give to thy soul's monition heed ;
> Who spares himself will not succeed.

THE SICK-CHAMBER A TEMPLE.

CAN say with truth that many a sick-bed has been to me as a house of worship, and many a sick-chamber as a holy temple. As I lay in silence and inquired of the Lord, "What dost thou say?" I obtained an answer and always such a one as showed that, however terrible his frowns, there was a loving heart concealed behind. Usually it was some vain imagination, some high thought, which the heavenly Husbandman had in his eye ; and so I was enabled to hold a sacred colloquy with him, and my soul was at peace. In truth, a sick-bed is generally the place where the blessing of the Christian faith becomes specially manifest. While in the heart of a child of the world sickness breeds obstinacy, pride, and discontent, and so eventually, when it has passed away, leaves no fruit, the contrary happens with the child of God. In his hours of languishing the mysteries of God's love and the unsearchable depths of his wisdom are properly disclosed. Such a silent sick-room sets a man once more loose from the world and its attachments, and from all courtship of human favor and human praise, and sends him back into life with a new and single eye.

Alas! I am conscious to myself how suddenly and deceitfully self-love can creep back into a heart which has been sanctified by faith ; therefore it is that I fervently pray, "Keep me in safety, O Lord, and let not my last state be worse than my first. Behold I myself implore of thee to humble me."

ONE WITH CHRIST.

BEFORE I had learned the nature of grace, I paused at this saying of the apostle, " I live, yet not I, but Christ liveth in me; " and I asked myself, What strange fancy of the Jewish rabbi is this? Does he really imagine that the Messias, who has been exalted to heaven, is now living in him? Yet true it is, that he who ascended up on high, and sitteth on the right hand of the Father, did likewise continue to abide with his followers upon earth, and has become the life of their life. Nor is this merely as when we say to a friend, " I still have thee in my heart," meaning thereby, " in my remembrance "; for, if it were so, how could the Saviour have told his disciples, " I go away, and come again unto you "? Or how could he have prayed " that they all may be one; as thou, Father, art in me, and I in thee, that they also may be one in us; that the world may believe that thou hast sent me; and the glory which thou gavest me I have given them, *that they may be one, even as we are one* "? Could he have said, " Where two or three are met together in my name, there am I in the midst of them," if the phrase " in my name " signified nothing more than " in remembrance of me "? No doubt, to remember the Lord is to stretch out a hand toward him. But the Lord must fill it. And this is done when, along with the Father, he takes up his abode with his children; when in his glorified humanity he draws near to the souls which seek him; and, finally, when in the celebration of the holy sacrament he makes them partake of and feed upon him.

THE CURE OF SELF-CONCEIT.

THE clearer the Christian's recognition of his union with the Lord, the more freely can he speak of what the Lord has enabled him to accomplish, be the things ever so great.

'T was grace that did it all, he says,
And claims not for himself the praise.

He who still hesitates to speak of his own works shows thereby that in what he does he thinks too much about himself; whereas the man who is firmly rooted in the article of grace, and who constantly bears about with him the consciousness of being one of the Lord's members, relates only the doings of the Lord when he is relating his own. Would a child have any sense of self-conceit when telling with a light heart all the fine things which he had purchased with the money given him by his father? There is a passage in which the apostle Paul avers, " I would not dare to speak of any of those things, if *Christ* had not wrought them by me, to make the Gentiles obedient by word and deed."[1] He did not hesitate, as many scrupulous people do, to say great things of himself, and bluntly avers, " I labored more abundantly than they all." To this, however, he appends in plain terms, " Yet not I, but the grace of God that was with me." And no doubt upon every occasion of his boasting the same idea was present to his mind. The rule, however, is, that the soul does not usually think much of its own work, unless it happen that some one calls it to account, or refuses to pay due honor to the work of God within us.

[1] Rom. 15: 18, Luther's version.

GOD'S WORK AND OURS.

THOU encouragest us by thy Word, saying, " Work out your own salvation with fear and trembling, for it is God who worketh in you both to will and to do of his good pleasure." How wonderfully in this text hast thou interwoven thy work with ours! With so holy earnestness dost thou enjoin us to work out our own salvation, that we expect nothing else than to be told that the power both to will and to do it is in our own hand. But no; rather dost thou incite us to work by the thought that both our willing and doing proceed from thee. And in this, O heavenly wisdom, I understand thy purpose. O, how much holier men would be if they would but receive with fear and trembling the yearnings and impulses in their bosoms, as if these were the heralds of a mighty monarch who brings a blessing with him where he is welcomed, but where he is repulsed leaves behind him a curse! The longing of a human soul after thee is thy boon; and when a mortal spirit yearns for God, it is a proof that God has already yearned for it. Even an Eastern poet could say: —

"Each ' Lord, appear,' thy lips pronounce, contains my ' Here
        am I ' —
A special messenger I send, veiled in thine every sigh;
Thy love is but a girdle of the love I bear to thee,
And sleeping in thy ' Come, O Lord,' there lies ' Here, son,'
        from me."

THE SACREDNESS OF SOLITUDE.

O GOD, how sacred to me were the hours which I spent in solitude with thee! My soul emerged from them as if from a bath. During its daily avocations, life with its multitudinous sounds rushes past like a roaring waterfall, deafening our ears so that we cannot understand ourselves, nor even God, when he speaks to us. How differently do all things appear, how different we appear to ourselves, when, after the bustle of the day, sacred and silent night has crept on! Then do voices within and around us, which before found no articulate words, begin to speak. Often, however, these voices are painful to the hearer, and therefore it is that he flies from hours of solitude. But shut not thine ears, dear reader: among them there is many a voice that calls thee home, and such a voice is always sad. But wilt thou, for no better reason than merely to spare thyself a touch of homesickness, try to forget in this far country that thou *hast* a home elsewhere? That is not wise, for so a time will come when even at home thou wilt appear a stranger. Seek to be alone with thyself. Every season of solitude is as a silent night, in which, when the din of this world dies away, boding voices from another begin to sound.

CONVERSING WITH GOD.

IN a house in which the mortar was dropping from the walls, and the rafters were beginning to break, there lived a man who was so deeply absorbed in his business that to one of his friends who sought to speak with him alone in order to warn him of his danger, he answered, "I have no time." Thou laughest at his folly, but thou art thyself the fool. Believe me, dear reader, unconscious of it although thou art, thy business is more important to thee than thyself; for otherwise how couldst thou decline when the voice of thy heavenly Friend bids thee retire with him, that he may inform thee about thyself and thine earthly tabernacle? Thou hast a certain feeling, though thou wilt not own it to thyself, that thou art not well, and yet thou shunnest so much as even an interview with thy Physician. Can that help thee? No; it helps thee nothing. Poor blinded man! From the loud tumult of life thou wilt be hurried unexpectedly away, and then thou wilt be brought into a solitude where the voices from which thou didst here endeavor to escape must of necessity be heard. Here they were the voices of a *friend;* there they will be the voice of thy *Judge.*

> To thy soul's inmost shrine repair,
> And there with God converse and dwell;
> To him that knows that palace fair
> The world will seem a prison cell.

THE JOY OF RECONCILIATION.

CONSIDER, O my soul, how great an honor thou contemnest in order to pursue a paltry enjoyment. Thou hastenest in all directions to visit men; and thy God is waiting for thee within, and thou permittest him to wait. Thou wouldst shun this most honorable of interviews far less, hadst thou but experienced the kindness and condescension with which on such occasions he communes with the soul. No doubt he has many things with which to upbraid it, but he upbraids with such gentleness and patience that all one can do is silently to weep tears of shame. On the other hand, he has likewise so many blessed things to tell the soul about its native land and home and the thoughts of peace which he cherishes on our behalf, and intends in the future to carry into effect, that it is good to be with him. Thou imaginest that he comes only to judge and punish, and knowest not that he comes also to pardon and to save, and that at every such absolution a festival is celebrated in the inmost recess of the soul, on which even the angels of heaven look down with delight.

A feast of joy that never ends
Is theirs whom Jesus deigns to own,
Gives them his peace, and calls his friends,
And to them all his grace makes known.

WHAT IS PRAYER?

O THOU sweet light of love, shine into my heart, so that even now in this poor life I may often celebrate with thee a peaceful Sabbath, and enjoy thy company in the fellowship of eternity.

> 'T was once my way to set apart
>   Both place and time for secret prayer;
> Now pray I always in my heart,
>   And am alone though anywhere.

This is what the apostle means when he admonishes us to pray without ceasing, and in such prayers all words and brisk emotions of the heart are for the time in suspense. Such prayers issue calmly forth, being in this respect like the solar light, whose approach we cannot hear, but which is yet accompanied by a warmth that testifies its presence. Yes, there is a deep, hidden colloquy of holy souls with God, which never ceases any more than does the beating of the pulse in a living man. It consists in an inward tending and aspiring of the soul toward its Source, and, although calm and silent, it influences and governs all the thoughts and volitions of him in whom it takes place. There are instances of the earth sending up from its lowest depths a tepid breath, scarcely perceptible to our senses, but which permeates the waters upon its surface, and impregnates them with medicinal virtues. And it is even so with the prayer peculiar to the man of piety; it hinders him in none of his avocations; rather, where it obtains, do these all thrive and prosper.

THE SECRET OF PRAYER.

WHAT a noble pattern might not St. Paul have been to me! At the time when thou wert laying the foundation stone of thy church, he had beheld thine arm visibly stretched forth from heaven. He had had actual experience that at thy nod the earth quaked and the fetters that bound thy servants broke asunder. Although, however, he had in many ways actually seen the working of thy miraculous hand, yet never once did he crave from thee its help. For two long years he wore his chains in the prison of Cæsarea, and in that of Rome for even a still longer period, and yet we do not read of his ever having either asked or expected of thee to work a miracle for his release. In complete resignation, he left it for the Lord to determine whether he was to depart this life or to abide in the flesh, and whether he was to visit the brethren in the imperial city, or to have that desire of his heart unfulfilled.

And by the light which thou givest me, O my Lord, I also can now interpret the promises of thy word in but one sense, which is this, that the great object for which thy true disciples will ever pray is that thy kingdom may come; and therefore that they will set their heart upon nothing, except in so far as they consider it the means by which that object may be promoted.

THE TEMPTATION OF MIRACLE-
WORKING.

WHEN I reflect how great would be the tempta-
tion if such as I possessed, like Peter, the
power of saying to the lame, "Rise up and
walk," or like Paul to the evil spirits, "I
command thee to come out of her," I am afraid. And
yet to pray with success, in a special case of need, is
likewise a miracle. I am still, O Lord, in the lowest
class of thy school, and for one who has never yet learned
rightly to believe in many of the manifest miracles of thy
grace, the power to work miracles would be an unsuit-
able gift. If perchance it shall ever happen that I am
deemed worthy of so great a distinction, it will only be
when I shall have learned to pray wholly in thy name.
And this I shall never learn until I have fully sacrificed
to thee all will of my own. For the present, dear Master, my prayer shall be : —

> Grant me the wonders of thy grace
>   In every day's events to see ;
> Thou meetest me in all my ways, —
>   O that I sought to meet with thee !
>
> Better to trust thy hand of might,
>   Even when by sable clouds concealed,
> Than own it when, to sense and sight,
>   Stretched forth from heaven, it stands
>   revealed.
>
> O help me then by faith to live,
>   The faith that to the unseen cleaves,
> Sure that eternity will give
>   Vision to him who here believes.

THE SCHOOL OF PATIENCE.

N truth, from no scrutiny of the heart, however deep it may go, can we ascertain that we do believe. It is only trial that can teach us this. In the parable of the sower we are told that not till "the sun was up" was it discovered that the seed had no root; and it is even so with faith. No man can know whether that noble plant has struck its roots in the better world, until the sun of tribulation has risen and shot down its scorching rays upon his head. Patience must have had her perfect work, must have endured unto the end, before all the fair virtues, which James calls fruits of the wisdom from above, can appear in the Christian's character, making him "pure, peaceable, gentle, and easy to be entreated, full of mercy and good fruits, without partiality, and without hypocrisy." I find in all Christians who have passed through much tribulation a certain quality of ripeness, which I am of opinion can be acquired in no other school. Just as a certain degree of solar heat is necessary to bring the finest sorts of fruit to perfection, so is the fiery trial indispensable for ripening the inner man. Claudius calls the Christian who has been subjected to it "the man with the moonbeam on his face." It is night that gives their brilliancy to the stars; and in like manner the night of adversity spreads over the countenance of the Christian who has endured it a strange cast, which bespeaks itself to be of the other world, and enforces reverence.

THE PRUNING-KNIFE.

OF all the suckers on his vine, there are none which the heavenly Husbandman endeavors with so intent an aim to prune away as those of pride, for he knows that into them the whole strength of the stock is most apt to run, wasting the generous sap, and thereby marring the goodly fruit. And hence the more the wilful heart rebels under the first little cross, and attempts to shake it off, the sooner does the Lord impose a second and then a third, until the lesson of submission has been learned. It is a beautiful rule which a pious servant of God has given us in the following words : —

> " If sickness, want, or dire mischance
> Are down upon thee poured,
> Fall on thy knees, and ask at once,
> What means thy message, Lord?
>
> " And if, my child, thou humbly take
> His answer to thy heart,
> Be sure that he will quickly make
> Thy troubles all depart."

If the soul in such a case inquires uprightly, it will not tarry long for an answer. An answer is generally given, and comes in clear and intelligible terms. And what is its drift? In nine cases out of ten it is at some devil of pride which has crept into the heart that the rod of God has been aimed.

HOW TO KNOW GOD'S WILL.

N my opinion, there are two things which ought to be taken to heart by those who desire to know the will of God aright, in order in all things to serve him alone. In the first place, it seems to me important that when we are in doubt and enter our closets to inquire of him, we should go with an undistracted heart, and be silent before him. "Come and bow down," must thou say to thyself, and bring before the face of the Omnipresent thy heart in a calm and gentle frame, with no bias either to the right hand or the left.

Enter thy closet, man, for there the sun of grace shines
     bright,
And there God opens wide his heart, to give life, joy, and
     light.
You only intercept the rays by word or act of thine,
Even to thy thought and will give pause, and wait the im-
     pulse divine ;
Let all within thee for the time be hushed in calm repose ;
'T is on the lake's unruffled breast the sun its image throws.

If at the time of prayer thy heart be thus a placid mirror, then for certain the answer to thy petitions will not come from thyself; thou wilt receive it from the Master.

In the second place, it is by "use" alone that we acquire "senses exercised to discern good and evil," and hence our rule must be to draw from God's word more and more deeply every day. No tree falls at the first stroke, and "to him that hath shall be given."

THE BEAUTY OF HUMILITY.

WE need do nothing but begin comparing ourselves with others, and pride instantly makes
its appearance afresh. The apostle says,
"Let every man prove his own work, and
then shall he have rejoicing in himself alone, and not
in another." There can be no doubt that the reason
why our Saviour was so fond of children was that
they are without self-conceit. When his disciples inquired which of them would be greatest in the kingdom of heaven, he called a little child unto him, and
set him in the midst of them, and said: "Verily I say
unto you, Except ye be converted, and become as little
children, ye shall not enter into the kingdom of heaven.
Whosoever, therefore, shall humble himself as this little
child, the same is the greatest in the kingdom of heaven."
The child does not compare, exercises little reflection,
looks neither to the right nor left, and the son of a king
will play with a beggar's boy without thinking of his
dignity at all. Now the longer a man frequents the
school of Jesus, the more he learns to keep in his own
path, to commit to the Lord, whose servants they are,
the task of pronouncing judgment upon others, to ab-
stain from all comparisons, and to go with his burden
to the Lord in prayer. How beautiful it is to see true
Christian humility gladdening the eyes of all others, but
unconscious of its own brightness! In fact, what
lovelier spectacle can be presented to the view of men
or angels than a disciple of Jesus ever employed in
covering the glowing embers of charity beneath the
ashes of self-abasement?

THE GOVERNMENT OF OUR LIVES.

MUST come to a clear decision of the question, Who is to have the government of my life? Alas! I have hitherto had too many masters, and not one supreme; for how can I affirm that any one is my master whose commandments are not the rule by which I walk? Every morning we ought afresh calmly and clearly to determine who our rightful master is, and then *turn our back to the world, and our face to Christ.* Unless we have firmly and unalterably resolved on this, it will from time to time happen, that when the world issues its command on the right hand and Christ his on the left, we will sometimes hold to the one master and despise the other. In nothing have I experienced the truth of this so much as in the matter of *men-pleasing.* It is amazing how much our thoughts and purposes and whole position depend upon our fellow men. Even the influence that the place and time at which we happen to live exerts upon our opinions and acts, is ultimately determined by some particular person. When, for example, I figure myself residing in another neighborhood, and among other influential people, I have the conviction that then many things would appear to me in a very different light from that in which I see them now. Does not much of the disquietude of the soul originate in the circumstance that, instead of seeking to please one, we seek to please many? In this way we become too external, and the quiet and sacred fire, which ought ever to burn for God upon the altar of the heart, is extinguished.

A CHRISTIAN'S RIGHTS.

HRISTIAN humility will not throw herself away, and never appear but in the guise of a miserable sinner; because He in whose school we have all been made miserable sinners has likewise made us children of God, — in the exercise of free *grace*, no doubt, and not for the merit of our works, that no flesh may boast. Christian humility will not throw itself away because occasions may come which require a Christian to avouch and vindicate both what and how much grace has been bestowed upon him. Not in vain has it been recorded that St. Paul asserted his right to the privileges of a Roman citizen; and as members of Christ and subjects of his kingdom we also have rights and prerogatives. Generally, indeed, the humble disciple of Jesus walks through life with a bent rather than with an uplifted head, like a tree loaded with fruit. When the occasion emerges, however, he, too, can hold his head up like others. He does not, indeed, either say or sing much about the gifts and graces he has received, just as full vessels differ from empty ones by the feebler sound which they emit. But where the case calls for it, he also can cheerfully sing and play, not indeed to his own, but to his Master's, glory. Under the purifying influence of the Spirit of Christ, we reach a point at which in childlike simplicity we can be conscious of, and are able also, if need be, to assert, the gifts we have received.

GODLIKE TRUTH.

DOES God ever pretend to be other than he is? Are not all his ways truth? God himself is truth, and he who sins against truth sins against God. That is enough to make the word of truth sacred to me. I need none of the arguments which others allege, such as that our Maker has given speech to man in order that it might be the picture of his thought, and that therefore lying is a sin against the purpose of God and the use for which speech was destined; that it is an abuse of confidence towards our neighbor. These arguments may be good in their place. Enough for me to say with David, " O Lord, thou art God, and thy words be true "; and, being the servant of the Lord, I will walk on no other path but his. Moreover, I see what becomes of those who try to bargain for an abatement of the truth. The stone cannot be stopped which has once begun to roll down the hill, and one lie produces seven. If you are to consider good reasons a sufficient excuse for passing off a lie, ah me! how cheap these are, especially when furnished by a wicked heart! I never saw a thief use his light fingers who had not good reasons to plead for doing so, although the only true one might have been that his fingers itched. Let the conscience have become so relaxed as to sell its consent for what are called good reasons, and I know of nothing which it will not sell. Rather will I say with the poet: —

> " The conscience which men pliant call,
> Is much the same as none at all."

THE TRIVIAL ROUND.

THE better and more serviceable the articles are which one Christian furnishes to another, the wholesomer the bread which the baker bakes, the more firmly the architect lays the foundation of the house which he builds, the more expeditiously and largely the merchant procures the commodities of other countries for the use and benefit of his own, — the more in such external services will a regard for the welfare, and a desire in all respects to consult the interests, of his brother be manifested. If all this spring from a desire to serve God and his neighbor, his daily work will be a work of Christian charity, and he will no longer require to wait for special and select occasions to exercise that virture. Luther has said that a married wife ought to be convinced that in her position the suckling of her babe and the tending of her children are as certainly acceptable to God as if he had spoken to her, and expressly commanded her to do it. In like manner, the servant girl who sweeps the house, boils the pot, and feeds the cattle, ought to be firmly persuaded in her mind that she is walking according to the divine commandment, if in these things she faithfully executes the orders she has received. And thus ought all ranks of men to cherish the confidence that it is God that has allotted to them their several trades and occupations, and to be contented each with his own, however bad it may be. In that case faith would place all of them on a level, for God pays no regard to whether thine be mean or noble, but only to whether thou acceptest it as allotted to thee by him.

DAILY TOIL A PREPARATION.

HAVE often, and with my whole heart, wished to know how much of the business and toil of the present life will be translated with us into the new heaven and new earth. A great man has said that " all we have learned in this world will be of no more use to us when we depart out of it than the names of the streets of London." I do not know, however, if that be true. It may well be that we think too meanly of the earthly creatures, as of all sublunary things; and that, when the dead shall rise, much of the business and employments which they followed here below will rise along with them, and take a nobler shape. Nay, might it not be said that, were the sweat wiped from the brow and sin extirpated from the heart, the work of earth might be a work of heaven? The more we contemplate them from this point of view, the higher the notion we will be ready to entertain of our pastimes here below. But for the present I agree with Luther, who said that, when he hung as a suckling on his mother's breast, little did he know what he was afterwards to eat or drink, or what manner of life he would lead; and far less do we understand how all that will be in the world to come. In this matter I will patiently wait, like the children on Christmas Eve, who with hearts full of confidence and hope stand behind the door until the time comes for it to be opened, and the tree, with its hundred lights and all the appendages about and upon it, bursts upon their eye and fully satisfies their heart; meanwhile, I will give heed to the apostle's advice, and " use this life as not abusing it."

WHAT WE SHALL BE.

HERE is, in fact, an eternal centre of spirits emitting innumerable rays, and on some particular one of these does every spirit reach that centre. For this reason, when congregated there, they shall all take part in the same hallelujah, and yet each with a voice and a tone peculiar to himself.

Almighty God, in whose hand it is to acquit or to condemn, I cannot but acknowledge thy full and perfect right to condemn me; and yet thou hast awarded me an inheritance so great that I scarcely dare for very shame to lift my eyes toward it. I should praise and thank thee through eternity, even though the place allotted me were on the remotest confine of thy holy land, or only at the threshold of thy heavenly temple. But thy word distinctly tells me that thou wilt draw me to thy heart, that thou wilt seat me on thy throne, and make me a copy of the brightness of thy glory. O give me faith sufficiently great and powerful to grasp so inconceivable a promise. At such a thought how does this little earth, with all its mighty woe, recede far, far behind me!

Here dwell forever joy and light.
The soul is clad in raiment bright
        Of spotless purity.
Like kings we sit on thrones, and wear
Immortal chaplets, fresh and fair,
        While changeless time rolls by.
O happy they that day who see,
When all and in all God shall be.

NO MORE TEARS.

"ND God shall wipe away all tears from their eyes; and there shall be no more death, neither sorrow, nor crying, neither shall there be any more pain; for the former things are passed away."

Here below we walk from day to day amid tears and want and death and sorrow and pain, and it might well appear as if human life could not exist without this bitter accompaniment; and yet every one feels in his inmost heart that it cannot and will not be thus forever. But if the word of God did not attest the fact, we could not venture to trust solely to the voice of the heart, for are not our hopes often the mere offspring of our wishes? Now, however, we know it. A day will come on which by all to whom grace has been given to believe in the Son of God, the toil and tears of the past shall be remembered no more. Up then, disconsolate hearts! whatever may be the burden which at present weighs you down. Look forward to the future, in which all sufferings shall be as if submerged in a mighty ocean. "Former things are passed away," says the voice of the prophet. The whole period of the world's history to which affliction and sorrow belonged shall lie behind us like a morning dream, and no remnant of it be left but that "peaceful fruit of righteousness" which is the growth of correction.

www.ingramcontent.com/pod-product-compliance
Lightning Source LLC
Chambersburg PA
CBHW030305030426
42337CB00012B/597